AF866351

Understanding Capital and Interest

Understanding Capital and Interest

With the Classic "What Is Money?"

M. Frederic Bastiat

Stonewell Press

ISBN 978-1-62730-091-9

The views expressed in this book are the responsibility of the author and do not necessarily represent the position of Stonewell Press. The reader alone is responsible for the use of any ideas or information provided by this book.

Published by Stonewell Press, Salt Lake City, Utah.

Any additions to original text © 2013 by Stonewell Press. All rights reserved. Printed in the United States of America.

Stonewell Press™ and the Stonewell Press logo are trademarks of Stonewell Press.

www.stonewellpress.com
editor@stonewellpress.com

Publisher's Preface

Frederic Bastiat (1801–1850) is viewed by some as one of the foremost political economists of all time. A native of France, his works were originally written in the French language. Even though his name has been largely forgotten in many circles, his philosophies continue to have a great influence on libertarians, free-market advocates, classical liberals, fiscal conservatives, and those who argue in favor of a limited government.

He wrote for the common man, earnestly seeking to be understood while also desiring to entertain to maintain reader interest. His discussions of money, capital, government, free trade, and the law are so concise and powerful that they have sometimes thoroughly persuaded those who initially held a completely opposite viewpoint. His philosophies for the most part are compatible with John Locke and Adam Smith. His philosophical heirs have included F. A. Hayek, Ludwig von Mises, and Milton Friedman.

Bastiat's works include *Essays on Political Economy, What Is Free Trade?, Economic Harmonies,* and the ever-popular *The Law.*

Even though some of the arguments of this book are presented in Bastiat's historical context, the principles discussed are as timely as the day they were written.

Bastiat tragically died of tuberculosis at the premature age of forty-nine.

CONTENTS

Understanding Capital and Interest

My object in this treatise is to examine the real nature of the Interest of Capital, for the purpose of proving that it is lawful, and explaining why it should be perpetual. This may appear singular, and yet, I confess, I am more afraid of being too plain than too obscure. I am afraid I may weary the reader by a series of mere truisms. But it is no easy matter to avoid this danger, when the facts with which we have to deal are known to every one by personal, familiar, and daily experience.

But, then, you will say, "What is the use of this treatise? Why explain what everybody knows?"

But, although this problem appears at first sight so very simple, there is more in it than you might suppose. I shall endeavour to prove this by an example. Mondor lends an instrument of labour to-day, which will be entirely destroyed in a week, yet the capital will not produce the less interest to Mondor or his heirs, through all eternity. Reader, can you honestly say that you understand the reason of this?

It would be a waste of time to seek any satisfactory explanation from the writings of economists. They have not thrown much light upon the reasons of the existence of interest. For this they are not to be blamed; for at the time they wrote, its lawfulness was not called in question. Now, however, times are altered; the case is different. Men, who consider themselves to be in advance of their age, have organised an active crusade against capital and interest; it is the productiveness of capital which they are attacking; not certain abuses in the administration of it, but the principle itself.

A journal has been established to serve as a vehicle for this crusade. It is conducted by M. Proudhon, and has, it is said, an immense circulation. The first number of this periodical contains the electoral manifesto of the *people.* Here we read, "The productiveness of capital, which is condemned by Christianity under the name of usury, is the true cause of misery, the true principle of destitution, the eternal obstacle to the establishment of the Republic."

Another journal, *La Ruche Populaire,* after having said some excellent things on labour, adds, "But, above all, labour ought to be free; that is, it ought to be organised in such a manner, *that money-lenders and patrons, or masters, should not be paid* for this liberty of labour, this right of labour, which is raised to so high a price by the traffickers of men." The only thought that I notice here, is that expressed by the words in italics, which imply a denial of the right to interest. The remainder of the article explains it.

It is thus that the democratic Socialist, Thore expresses himself:—

"The revolution will always have to be recommenced, so long as we occupy ourselves with consequences only, without having the logic or the courage to attack the principle itself. This principle is capital, false property, interest, and usury, which by the old *regime,* is made to weigh upon labour.

"Ever since the aristocrats invented the incredible fiction, *that capital possesses the power of reproducing itself,* the workers have been at the mercy of the idle.

"At the end of a year, will you find an additional crown in a bag of one hundred shillings? At the end of fourteen years, will your shillings have doubled in your bag?

"Will a work of industry or of skill produce another, at the end of fourteen years?

"Let us begin, then, by demolishing this fatal fiction."

I have quoted the above, merely for the sake of establishing the fact, that many persons consider the productiveness of capital a false, a fatal, and an iniquitous principle. But quotations are superfluous; it is well known that the people attribute their sufferings to what they call *the trafficking in man by man.* In fact, the phrase, *tyranny of capital,* has become proverbial.

I believe there is not a man in the world, who is aware of the whole importance of this question:—

"Is the interest of capital natural, just, and lawful, and as useful to the payer as to the receiver?"

You answer, No; I answer, Yes. Then we differ entirely; but it is of the utmost importance to discover which of us is in the right, otherwise we shall incur the danger of making a false solution of the question, a matter of opinion. If the error is on my side, however, the evil would not be so great. It must be inferred that I know nothing about the true interests of the masses, or the march of human progress; and that all my arguments are but as so many grains of sand, by which the car of the revolution will certainly not be arrested.

But if, on the contrary, M. Proudhon and Thore are deceiving themselves, it follows that they are leading the people astray—that they are showing them the evil where it does not exist; and thus giving a false direction to their ideas, to their antipathies, to their dislikes, and to their attacks. It follows that the misguided people are rushing into a horrible and absurd struggle, in which victory would be more fatal than defeat; since, according to this supposition, the result would be the realisation of universal evils, the destruction of every means of emancipation, the consummation of its own misery.

This is just what M. Proudhon has acknowledged, with perfect good faith. "The foundation stone," he told me, "of my system is the *gratuitousness of credit.* If I am mistaken in this, Socialism is a vain dream." I add, it is a dream, in which the people are tearing themselves to pieces. Will it, therefore, be a cause for surprise, if, when they awake, they find themselves mangled and bleeding? Such a danger as this is enough to justify me fully, if, in the course of the discussion, I allow myself to be led into some trivialities and some prolixity.

Capital and Interest

I address this treatise to the workmen of Paris, more especially to those who have enrolled themselves under the banner of Socialist democracy. I proceed to consider these two questions:—

1st. Is it consistent with the nature of things, and with justice, that capital should produce interest?

2nd. Is it consistent with the nature of things, and with justice, that the interest of capital should be perpetual?

The working men of Paris will certainly acknowledge that a more important subject could not be discussed.

Since the world began, it has been allowed, at least in part, that capital ought to produce interest. But latterly it has been affirmed, that herein lies the very social error which is the cause of pauperism and inequality. It is, therefore, very essential to know now on what ground we stand.

For if levying interest from capital is a sin, the workers have a right to revolt against social order, as it exists. It is in vain to tell them that they ought to have recourse to legal and pacific means: it would be a hypocritical recommendation. When on the one side there is a strong man, poor, and a victim of robbery—on the other, a weak man, but rich, and a robber—it is singular enough that we should say to the former, with a hope of persuading him, "Wait till your oppressor voluntarily renounces oppression, or till it shall cease of itself." This cannot be; and those who tell us that capital is by nature unproductive, ought to know that they are provoking a terrible and immediate struggle.

If, on the contrary, the interest of capital is natural, lawful, consistent with the general good, as favourable to the borrower as to the lender, the economists who deny it, the tribunes who traffic in this pretended social wound, are leading the workmen into a senseless and unjust struggle, which can have no other issue than the misfortune of all. In fact, they are arming labour against capital. So much the better, if these two powers are really antagonistic; and may the struggle soon be ended! But, if they are in harmony, the struggle is the greatest evil which can be inflicted on society. You see, then, workmen, that there is not a more important question than this:—"Is the interest of capital lawful or not?" In the former case, you must immediately renounce the struggle to which you are being urged; in the second, you must carry it on bravely, and to the end.

Productiveness of capital—perpetuity of interest. These are difficult questions. I must endeavour to make myself clear. And for that purpose I shall have recourse to example rather than to demonstration; or rather, I shall place the demonstration in the example. I begin by acknowledging that, at first sight, it may appear strange that capital should pretend to a remuneration, and above all, to a perpetual remuneration. You will say,

"Here are two men. One of them works from morning till night, from one year's end to another; and if he consumes all which he has gained, even by superior energy, he remains poor. When Christmas comes he is no forwarder than he was at the beginning of the year, and has no other prospect but to begin again. The other man does nothing, either with his hands or his head; or at least, if he makes use of them at all, it is only for his own pleasure; it is allowable for him to do nothing, for he has an income. He does not work, yet he lives well; he has everything in abundance; delicate dishes, sumptuous furniture, elegant equipages; nay, he even consumes, daily, things which the workers have been obliged to produce by the sweat of their brow, for these things do not make themselves; and, as far as he is concerned, he has had no hand in their production. It is the workmen who have caused this corn to grow, polished this furniture, woven these carpets; it is our wives and daughters who have spun, cut out, sewed, and embroidered these stuffs. We work, then, for him and for ourselves; for him first, and then for ourselves, if there is anything left. But here is something more striking still. If the former of these two men, the worker, consumes within the year any profit which may have been left him in that year, he is always at the point from which he started, and his destiny condemns him to move incessantly in a perpetual circle, and a monotony of exertion. Labour, then, is rewarded only once. But if the other, the 'gentleman,' consumes his yearly income in the year, he has, the year after, in those which follow, and through all eternity, an income always equal, inexhaustible, *perpetual.* Capital, then, is remunerated, not only once or twice, but an indefinite number of times! So that, at the end of a hundred years, a family which has placed 20,000 francs,[1] at five per cent., will have had 100,000 francs; and this will not prevent it from having 100,000 more, in the following century. In other words, for 20,000 francs, which represent its labour, it will have levied, in two centuries, a tenfold value on the labour of others. In this social arrangement, is there not a monstrous evil to be reformed? And this is not all. If it should please this family to curtail its enjoyments a little—to spend, for example, only 900 francs, instead of 1,000—it may, without any labour, without any other trouble beyond that of investing 100 francs a year, increase its capi-

1. A franc is 10d. of our money.

tal and its income in such rapid progression, that it will soon be in a position to consume as much as a hundred families of industrious workmen. Does not all this go to prove that society itself has in its bosom a hideous cancer, which ought to be eradicated at the risk of some temporary suffering?"

These are, it appears to me, the sad and irritating reflections which must be excited in your minds by the active and superficial crusade which is being carried on against capital and interest. On the other hand, there are moments in which, I am convinced, doubts are awakened in your minds, and scruples in your conscience. You say to yourselves sometimes, "But to assert that capital ought not to produce interest, is to say that he who has created instruments of labour, or materials, or provisions of any kind, ought to yield them up without compensation. Is that just? And then, if it is so, who would lend these instruments, these materials, these provisions? who would take care of them? who even would create them? Every one would consume his proportion, and the human race would never advance a step. Capital would be no longer formed, since there would be no interest in forming it. It would become exceedingly scarce. A singular step towards gratuitous loans! A singular means of improving the condition of borrowers, to make it impossible for them to borrow at any price! What would become of labour itself? for there will be no money advanced, and not one single kind of labour can be mentioned, not even the chase, which can be pursued without money in hand. And, as for ourselves, what would become of us? What! we are not to be allowed to borrow, in order to work in the prime of life, nor to lend, that we may enjoy repose in its decline? The law will rob us of the prospect of laying by a little property, because it will prevent us from gaining any advantage from it. It will deprive us of all stimulus to save at the present time, and of all hope of repose for the future. It is useless to exhaust ourselves with fatigue: we must abandon the idea of leaving our sons and daughters a little property, since modern science renders it useless, for we should become traffickers in men if we were to lend it on interest. Alas! the world which these persons would open before us, as an imaginary good, is still more dreary and desolate than that which they condemn, for hope, at any rate, is not banished from the latter." Thus, in all respects, and in every point of view, the question is a serious one. Let us hasten to arrive at a solution.

Our civil code has a chapter entitled, "On the manner of transmitting property." I do not think it gives a very complete nomenclature on this point. When a man by his labour has made some useful thing—in other words, when he has created a *value*—it can only pass into the hands of another by one of the following modes—as a gift, by the right of inheritance, by exchange, loan, or theft. One word upon each of these, except the last, although it plays a greater part in the world than we may think. A gift needs no definition. It is essentially voluntary and spontaneous. It depends exclusively upon the giver, and the receiver cannot be said to have any right to it. Without a doubt, morality and religion make it a duty for men, especially the rich, to deprive themselves voluntarily of that which they possess, in favour of their less fortunate brethren. But this is an entirely moral obligation. If it were to be asserted on principle, admitted in practice, or sanctioned by law, that every man has a right to the property of another, the gift would have no merit—charity and gratitude would be no longer virtues. Besides, such a doctrine would suddenly and universally arrest labour and production, as severe cold congeals water and suspends animation; for who would work if there was no longer to be any connection between labour and the satisfying of our wants? Political economy has not treated of gifts. It has hence been concluded that it disowns them, and that it is therefore a science devoid of heart. This is a ridiculous accusation. That science which treats of the laws resulting from the *reciprocity of services,* had no business to inquire into the consequences of generosity with respect to him who receives, nor into its effects, perhaps still more precious, on him who gives: such considerations belong evidently to the science of morals. We must allow the sciences to have limits; above all, we must not accuse them of denying or undervaluing what they look upon as foreign to their department.

The right of inheritance, against which so much has been objected of late, is one of the forms of gift, and assuredly the most natural of all. That which a man has produced, he may consume, exchange, or give. What can be more natural than that he should give it to his children? It is this power, more than any other, which inspires him with courage to labour and to save. Do you know why the principle of right of inheritance is thus called in question? Because it is imagined that the property thus transmitted is plundered from the masses. This is a fatal error. Political economy demonstrates, in the most peremptory manner, that all value produced is a creation which does no harm to any person whatever. For that reason it may be consumed, and, still more, transmitted, without hurting any one; but I shall not pursue these reflections, which do not belong to the subject.

Exchange is the principal department of political economy, because it is by far the most frequent method of transmitting property, according to the free and voluntary agreements of the laws and effects of which this science treats.

Properly speaking, exchange is the reciprocity of services. The parties say between themselves, "Give me this, and I will give you that"; or, "Do this for me, and I will do that for you." It is well to remark (for this will throw a new light on the notion of value) that the second form is always implied in the first. When it is said, "Do this for me, and I will do that for you," an exchange of service for service is proposed. Again, when it is said, "Give me this, and I will give you that," it is the same as saying, "I yield to you what I have done, yield to me what you have done." The labour is past, instead of present; but the exchange is not the less governed by the comparative valuation of the two services: so that it is quite correct to say that the principle of *value* is in the services rendered and received on account of the productions exchanged, rather than in the productions themselves.

We must remark, also, that the constant appearance of money in every exchange has overturned and misled all our ideas: men have ended in thinking that money was true riches, and that to multiply it was to multiply services and products. Hence the prohibitory system; hence paper money; hence the celebrated aphorism, "What one gains the other loses"; and all the errors which have ruined the earth, and embrued it with blood.[1] After much research it has been found, that in order to make the two services exchanged of equivalent value, and in order to render the exchange *equitable,* the best means was to allow it to be free. However plausible, at first sight, the intervention of the State might be, it was soon perceived that it is always oppressive to one or other of the contracting parties. When we look into these subjects, we are always compelled to rea-

1. This error will be combated in a pamphlet, entitled "Cursed Money."

son upon this maxim, that *equal value* results from liberty. We have, in fact, no other means of knowing whether, at a given moment, two services are of the same value, but that of examining whether they can be readily and freely exchanged. Allow the State, which is the same thing as force, to interfere on one side or the other, and from that moment all the means of appreciation will be complicated and entangled, instead of becoming clear. It ought to be the part of the State to prevent, and, above all, to repress artifice and fraud; that is, to secure liberty, and not to violate it. I have enlarged a little upon exchange, although loan is my principal object: my excuse is, that I conceive that there is in a loan an actual exchange, an actual service rendered by the lender, and which makes the borrower liable to an equivalent service,—two services, whose comparative value can only be appreciated, like that of all possible services, by freedom. Now, if it is so, the perfect lawfulness of what is called house-rent, farm-rent, interest, will be explained and justified. Let us consider the case of *loan.*In reality, services are scarcely ever exchanged directly. There is a medium, which is termed *money.* Paul has completed a coat, for which he wishes to receive a little bread, a little wine, a little oil, a visit from a doctor, a ticket for the play, &c. The exchange cannot be effected in kind, so what does Paul do? He first exchanges his coat for some money, which is called *sale;* then he exchanges this money again for the things which he wants, which is called *purchase;* and now, only, has the reciprocity of services completed its circuit; now, only, the labour and the compensation are balanced in the same individual,—"I have done this for society, it has done that for me." In a word, it is only now that the exchange is actually accomplished. Thus, nothing can be more correct than this observation of J. B. Say:—"Since the introduction of money, every exchange is resolved into two elements, *sale* and *purchase.* It is the reunion of these two elements which renders the exchange complete."

Suppose two men exchange two services or two objects, whose equal value is beyond all dispute. Suppose, for example, Peter says to Paul, "Give me ten sixpences, I will give you a five-shilling piece." We cannot imagine an equal value more unquestionable. When the bargain is made, neither party has any claim upon the other. The exchanged services are equal. Thus it follows, that if one of the parties wishes to introduce into the bargain an additional clause, advantageous to himself, but unfavourable to the other party, he must agree to a second clause, which shall re-establish the equilibrium, and the law of justice. It would be absurd to deny the justice of a second clause of compensation. This granted, we will suppose that Peter, after having said to Paul, "Give me ten sixpences, I will give you a crown," adds, "You shall give me the ten sixpences *now,* and I will give you the crown-piece *in a year";* it is very evident that this new proposition alters the claims and advantages of the bargain; that it alters the proportion of the two services. Does it not appear plainly enough, in fact, that Peter asks of Paul a new and an additional service; one of a different kind? Is it not as if he had said, "Render me the service of allowing me to use for my profit, for a year, five shillings which belong to you, and which you might have used for yourself?" And what good reason have you to maintain that Paul is bound to render this especial service gratuitously; that he has no right to demand anything more in consequence of this requisition; that the State ought to interfere to force him to submit? Is it not incomprehensible that the economist, who preaches such a doctrine to the people, can reconcile it with his principle of *the reciprocity of services?* Here I have introduced cash; I have been led to do so by a desire to place, side by side, two objects of exchange, of a perfect and indisputable equality of value. I was anxious to be prepared for objections; but, on the other hand, my demonstration would have been more striking still, if I had illustrated my principle by an agreement for exchanging the services or the productions themselves.

Suppose, for example, a house and a vessel of a value so perfectly equal that their proprietors are disposed to exchange them even-handed, without excess or abatement. In fact let the bargain be settled by a lawyer. At the moment of each taking possession, the shipowner says to the citizen, "Very well; the transaction is completed, and nothing can prove its perfect equity better than our free and voluntary consent. Our conditions thus fixed, I shall propose to you a little practical modification. You shall let me have your house to-day, but I shall not put you in possession of my ship for a year; and the reason I make this demand of you is, that, during this year of *delay,* I wish to use the vessel." That we may not be embarrassed by considerations relative to the deterioration of the thing lent, I will suppose the shipowner to add, "I will engage, at the end of the year, to hand over to you the vessel in the state in which it is to-day." I ask of every candid man, I ask of M. Proudhon himself, if the citizen has not a right to answer, "The new clause which you propose entirely alters the proportion or the equal value of the exchanged services. By it, I shall be deprived, for the space of a year, both at once of my house and of your vessel. By it, you will make use of both. If, in the absence of this clause, the bargain was just, for the same reason the clause is injurious to me. It stipulates for a loss to me, and a gain to you. You are requiring of me a new service; I have a right to refuse, or to require of you, as a compensation, an equivalent service." If the parties are agreed upon this compensation, the principle of which is incontestable, we can easily distinguish two transactions in one, two exchanges of service in one. First, there is the exchange of the house for the vessel; after this, there is the delay granted by one of the parties, and the compensation correspondent to this delay yielded by the other. These two new services take the generic and abstract names of *credit* and *interest.* But names do not change the nature of things; and I defy any one to dare to maintain that there exists here, when all is done, a service for a service, or a reciprocity of services. To say that one of these services does not challenge the other, to say that the first ought to be rendered gratuitously, without injustice, is to say that injustice consists in the reciprocity of services,—that justice consists in one of the parties giving and not receiving, which is a contradiction in terms.

To give an idea of interest and its mechanism, allow me to make use of two or three anecdotes. But, first, I must say a few words upon capital.

There are some persons who imagine that capital is money, and this is precisely the reason why they deny its productiveness; for, as M. Thore says, crowns are not endowed with the power of reproducing themselves. But it is not true that capital and money are the same thing. Before the discovery of the precious metals, there were capitalists in the world; and I venture to say that at that time, as now, everybody was a capitalist, to a certain extent.

What is capital, then? It is composed of three things:—

1st. Of the materials upon which men operate, when these materials have already a value communicated by some human effort, which has bestowed upon them the principle of remuneration—wool, flax, leather, silk, wood, &c.

2nd. Instruments which are used for working—tools, machines, ships, carriages, &c.

3rd. Provisions which are consumed during labour—victuals, stuffs, houses, &c.

Without these things the labour of man would be unproductive and almost void; yet these very things have required much work, especially at first. This is the reason that so much value has been attached to the possession of them, and also that it is perfectly lawful to exchange and to sell them, to make a profit of them if used, to gain remuneration from them if lent.

Now for my anecdotes.

The Sack of Corn

Mathurin, in other respects as poor as Job, and obliged to earn his bread by day-labour, became nevertheless, by some inheritance, the owner of a fine piece of uncultivated land. He was exceedingly anxious to cultivate it. "Alas!" said he, "to make ditches, to raise fences, to break the soil, to clear away the brambles and stones, to plough it, to sow it, might bring me a living in a year or two; but certainly not to-day, or to-morrow. It is impossible to set about farming it, without previously saving some provisions for my subsistence until the harvest; and I know, by experience, that preparatory labour is indispensable, in order to render present labour productive." The good Mathurin was not content with making these reflections. He resolved to work by the day, and to save something from his wages to buy a spade and a sack of corn; without which things, he must give up his fine agricultural projects. He acted so well, was so active and steady, that he soon saw himself in possession of the wished-for sack of corn. "I shall take it to the mill," said he, "and then I shall have enough to live upon till my field is covered with a rich harvest." Just as he was starting, Jerome came to borrow his treasure of him. "If you will lend me this sack of corn," said Jerome, "you will do me a great service; for I have some very lucrative work in view, which I cannot possibly undertake, for want of provisions to live upon until it is finished." "I was in the same case," answered Mathurin, "and if I have now secured bread for several months, it is at the expense of my arms and my stomach. Upon what principle of justice can it be devoted to the realisation of *your* enterprise instead of *mine?*"

You may well believe that the bargain was a long one. However, it was finished at length, and on these conditions:—

First—Jerome promised to give back, at the end of the year, a sack of corn of the same quality, and of the same weight, without missing a single grain. "This first clause is perfectly just," said he, "for without it Mathurin would *give,* and not *lend.*"

Secondly—He engaged to deliver *five litres* on *every hectolitre.* "This clause is no less just than the other," thought he; "for without it Mathurin would do me a service without compensation; he would inflict upon himself a privation—he would renounce his cherished enterprise—he would enable me to accomplish mine—he would cause me to enjoy for a year the fruits of his savings, and all this gratuitously. Since he delays the cultivation of his land, since he enables me to realise a lucrative labour, it is quite natural that I should let him partake, in a certain proportion, of the profits which I shall gain by the sacrifice he makes of his own."

On his side, Mathurin, who was something of a scholar, made this calculation:—"Since, by virtue of the first clause, the sack of corn will return to me at the end of a year," he said to himself, "I shall be able to lend it again; it will return to me at the end of the second year; I may lend it again, and so on, to all eternity. However, I cannot deny that it will have been eaten long ago. It is singular that I should be perpetually the owner of a sack of corn, although the one I have lent has been consumed for ever. But this is explained thus:—It will be consumed in the service of Jerome. It will put it into the power of Jerome to produce a superior value; and, consequently, Jerome will be able to restore me a sack of corn, or the value of it, without having suffered the slightest injury: but quite the contrary. And as regards myself, this value ought to be my property, as long as I do not consume it myself. If I had used it to clear my land, I should have received it again in the form of a fine harvest. Instead of that, I lend it, and shall recover it in the form of repayment.

"From the second clause, I gain another piece of information. At the end of the year I shall be in possession of five litres of corn over the one hundred that I have just lent. If, then, I were to continue to work by the day, and to save part of my wages, as I have been doing, in the course of time I should be able to lend two sacks of corn; then three; then four; and when I should have gained a sufficient number to enable me to live on these additions of five litres over and above each, I shall be at liberty to take a little repose in my old age. But how is this? In this case, shall I not be living at the expense of others? No, certainly, for it has been proved that in lending I perform a service; I complete the labour of my borrowers, and only deduct a trifling part of the excess of production, due to my lendings and savings. It is a marvellous thing that a man may thus realise a leisure which injures no one, and for which he cannot be envied without injustice."

The House

Mondor had a house. In building it, he had extorted nothing from any one whatever. He owed it to his own personal labour, or, which is the same thing, to labour justly rewarded. His first care was to make a bargain with an architect, in virtue of which, by means of a hundred crowns a year, the latter engaged to keep the house in constant good repair. Mondor was already congratulating himself on the happy days which he hoped to spend in this retreat, declared sacred by our Constitution. But Valerius wished to make it his residence.

"How can you think of such a thing?" said Mondor to Valerius. "It is I who have built it; it has cost me ten years of painful labour, and now you would enjoy it!" They agreed to refer the matter to judges. They chose no profound economists,—there were none such in the country. But they found some just and sensible men; it all comes to the same thing; political economy, justice, good sense, are all the same thing. Now here is the decision made by the judges:—If Valerius wishes to occupy Mondor's house for a year, he is bound to submit to three conditions. The first is to quit at the end of the year, and to restore the house in good repair, saving the inevitable decay resulting from mere duration. The second, to refund to Mondor the 300 francs which the latter pays annually to the architect to repair the injuries of time; for these injuries taking place whilst the house is in the service of Valerius, it is perfectly just that he should bear the consequences. The third, that he should render to Mondor a service equivalent to that which he receives. As to this equivalence of services, it must be freely discussed between Mondor and Valerius.

The Plane

A very long time ago there lived, in a poor village, a joiner, who was a philosopher, as all my heroes are in their way. James worked from morning till night with his two strong arms, but his brain was not idle for all that. He was fond of reviewing his actions, their causes, and their effects. He sometimes said to himself, "With my hatchet, my saw, and my hammer, I can make only coarse furniture, and can only get the pay for such. If I only had a *plane,* I should please my customers more, and they would pay me more. It is quite just; I can only expect services proportioned to those which I render myself. Yes! I am resolved, I will make myself a *plane.*"

However, just as he was setting to work, James reflected further:—"I work for my customers 300 days in the year. If I give ten to making my plane, supposing it lasts me a year, only 290 days will remain for me to make my furniture. Now, in order that I be not the loser in this matter, I must gain henceforth, with the help of the plane, as much in 290 days, as I now do in 300. I must even gain more; for unless I do so, it would not be worth my while to venture upon any innovations." James began to calculate. He satisfied himself that he should sell his finished furniture at a price which would amply compensate for the ten days devoted to the plane; and when no doubt remained on this point, he set to work. I beg the reader to remark, that the power which exists in the tool to increase the productiveness of labour, is the basis of the solution which follows.

At the end of ten days, James had in his possession an admirable plane, which he valued all the more for having made it himself. He danced for joy,—for, like the girl with her basket of eggs, he reckoned all the profits which he expected to derive from the ingenious instrument; but, more fortunate than she, he was not reduced to the necessity of saying goodbye to calf, cow, pig, and eggs, together. He was building his fine castles in the air, when he was interrupted by his acquaintance William, a joiner in the neighbouring village. William having admired the plane, was struck with the advantages which might be gained from it. He said to James:—

W. You must do me a service.

J. What service?

W. Lend me the plane for a year.

As might be expected, James at this proposal did not fail to cry out, "How can you think of such a thing, William? Well, if I do you this service, what will you do for me in return?"

W. Nothing. Don't you know that a loan ought to be gratuitous? Don't you know that capital is naturally unproductive? Don't you know fraternity has been proclaimed. If you only do me a service for the sake of receiving one from me in return, what merit would you have?

J. William, my friend, fraternity does not mean that all the sacrifices are to be on one side; if so, I do not see why they should not be on yours. Whether a loan should be gratuitous I don't know; but I do know that if I were to lend you my plane for a year it would be giving it you. To tell you the truth, that was not what I made it for.

W. Well, we will say nothing about the modern maxims discovered by the Socialist gentlemen. I ask you to do me a service; what service do you ask me in return?

J. First, then, in a year, the plane will be done for, it will be good for nothing. It is only just, that you should let me have another exactly like it; or that you should give me money enough to get it repaired; or that you should supply me the ten days which I must devote to replacing it.

W. This is perfectly just. I submit to these conditions. I engage to return it, or to let you have one like it, or the value of the same. I think you must be satisfied with this, and can require nothing further.

J. I think otherwise. I made the plane for myself, and not for you. I expected to gain some advantage from it, by my work being better finished and better paid, by an improvement in my condition. What reason is there that I should make the plane, and you should gain the profit? I might as well ask you to give me your saw and hatchet! What a confusion! Is it not natural that each should keep what he has made with his own hands, as well as his hands themselves? To use without recompense the hands of another, I call slavery; to use without recompense the plane of another, can this be called fraternity?

W. But, then, I have agreed to return it to you at the end of a year, as well polished and as sharp as it is now.

J. We have nothing to do with next year; we are speaking of this year. I have made the plane for the sake of improving my work and condition; if you merely return it to me in a year, it is you who will gain the profit of it during the whole of that time. I am not bound to do you such a service without receiving anything from you in return: therefore, if you wish for my plane, independently of the entire restoration already bargained for, you must do me a service which we will now discuss; you must grant me remuneration.

And this was done thus:—William granted a remuneration calculated in such a way that, at the end of the year, James received his plane quite new, and in addition, a compensation, consisting of a new plank, for the advantages of which he had deprived himself, and which he had yielded to his friend.

It was impossible for any one acquainted with the transaction to discover the slightest trace in it of oppression or injustice.

I maintain, first of all, that the *sack of corn* and the *plane* are here the type, the model, a faithful representation, the symbol of all capital; as the five litres of corn and the plank are the type, the model, the representation, the symbol of all interest. This granted, the following are, it seems to me, a series of consequences, the justice of which it is impossible to dispute.The singular part of it is, that, at the end of the year, the plane came into James's possession, and he lent it again; recovered it, and lent it a third and fourth time. It has passed into the hands of his son, who still lends it. Poor plane! how many times has it changed, sometimes its blade, sometimes its handle. It is no longer the same plane, but it has always the same value, at least for James's posterity. Workmen! let us examine into these little stories.

1st. If the yielding of a plank by the borrower to the lender is a natural, equitable, lawful remuneration, the just price of a real service, we may conclude that, as a general rule, it is in the nature of capital to produce interest. When this capital, as in the foregoing examples, takes the form of an *instrument of labour,* it is clear enough that it ought to bring an advantage to its possessor, to him who has devoted to it his time, his brains, and his strength. Otherwise, why should he have made it? No necessity of life can be immediately satisfied with instruments of labour; no one eats planes or drinks saws, except, indeed, he be a conjuror. If a man determines to spend his time in the production of such things, he must have been led to it by the consideration of the power which these instruments add to his power; of the time which they save him; of the perfection and rapidity which they give to his labour; in a word, of the advantages which they procure for him. Now, these advantages, which have been prepared by labour, by the sacrifice of time which might have been used in a more immediate manner, are we bound, as soon as they are ready to be enjoyed, to confer them gratuitously upon another? Would it be an advance in social order, if the law decided thus, and citizens should pay officials for causing such a law to be executed by force? I venture to say, that there is not one amongst you who would support it. It would be to legalize, to organize, to systematize injustice itself, for it would be proclaiming that there are men born to render, and others born to receive, gratuitous services. Granted, then, that interest is just, natural, and lawful.

2nd. A second consequence, not less remarkable than the former, and, if possible, still more conclusive, to which I call your attention, is this:—*Interest is not injurious to the borrower.* I mean to say, the obligation in which the borrower finds himself, to pay a remuneration for the use of capital, cannot do any harm to his condition. Observe, in fact, that James and William are perfectly free, as regards the transaction to which the plane gave occasion. The transaction cannot be accomplished without the consent of the one as well as of the other. The worst which can happen is, that James may be too exacting; and in this case, William, refusing the loan, remains as he was before. By the fact of his agreeing to borrow, he proves that he considers it an advantage to himself; he proves, that after every calculation, including the remuneration, whatever it may be, required of him, he still finds it more profitable to borrow than not to borrow. He only determines to do so because he has compared the inconveniences with the advantages. He has calculated that the day on which he returns the plane, accompanied by the remuneration agreed upon, he will have effected more work, with the same labour, thanks to this tool. A profit will remain to him, otherwise he would not have borrowed. The two services of which we are speaking are exchanged according to the law which governs all exchanges, the law of supply and demand. The claims of James have a natural and impassable limit. This is the point in which the remuneration demanded by him would absorb all the advantage which William might find in making use of a plane. In this case, the borrowing would not take place. William would be bound either to make a plane for himself, or to do without one, which would leave him in his original condition. He borrows, because he gains by borrowing. I know very well what will be told me. You will say, William may be deceived, or, perhaps, he may be governed by necessity, and be obliged to submit to a harsh law.

It may be so. As to errors in calculation, they belong to the infirmity of our nature, and to argue from this against the transaction in question, is objecting the possibility of loss in all imaginable transactions, in every human act. Error is an accidental fact, which is incessantly remedied by experience. In short, everybody must guard against it. As far as those hard necessities are concerned, which force persons to burdensome borrowings, it is clear that these necessities exist previously to the borrowing. If William is in a situation in which he cannot possibly do without a plane, and must borrow one at any price, does this situation result from James having taken the trouble to make the tool? Does it not exist independently of this circumstance? However harsh, however severe James may be, he will never render the supposed condition of William worse than it is. Morally, it is true, the lender will be to blame; but, in an economical point of view, the loan itself can never be considered responsible for previous necessities, which it has not created, and which it relieves to a certain extent.

But this proves something to which I shall return. The evident interests of William, representing here the borrowers, there are many Jameses and planes, in other words, lenders and capitals. It is very evident, that if William can say to James,—"Your demands are exorbitant; there is no lack of planes in the world"; he will be in a better situation than if James's plane was the only one to be borrowed. Assuredly, there is no maxim more true than this—service for service. But left us not forget that no service has a fixed and absolute value, compared with others. The contracting parties are free. Each carries his requisitions to the farthest possible point, and the most favourable circumstance for these requisitions is the absence of rivalship. Hence it follows, that if there is a class of men more interested than any other in the formation, multiplication, and abundance of capitals, it is mainly that of the borrowers. Now, since capitals can only be formed and increased by the stimulus and the prospect of remuneration, let this class understand the injury they are inflicting on themselves when they deny the lawfulness of interest, when they proclaim that credit should be gratuitous, when they declaim against the pretended tyranny of capital, when they discourage saving, thus forcing capitals to become scarce, and consequently interests to rise.

3rd. The anecdote I have just related enables you to explain this apparently singular phenomenon, which is termed the duration or perpetuity of interest. Since, in lending his plane, James has been able, very lawfully, to make it a condition that it should be returned to him, at the end of a year, in the same state in which it was when he lent it, is it not evident that he may, at the expiration of the term, lend it again on the same conditions? If he resolves upon the latter plan, the plane will return to him at the end of every year, and that without end. James will then be in a condition to lend it without end; that is, he may derive from it a perpetual interest. It will be said, that the plane will be worn out. That is true; but it will be worn out by the hand and for the profit of the borrower. The latter has taken into account this gradual wear, and taken upon himself, as he ought, the consequences. He has reckoned that he shall derive from this tool an advantage, which will allow him to restore it in its original condition, after having realised a profit from it. As long as James does not use this capital himself, or for his own advantage—as long as he renounces the advantages which allow it to be restored to its original condition—he will have an incontestable right to have it restored, and that independently of interest.

Observe, besides, that if, as I believe I have shown, James, far from doing any harm to William, has done him a *service* in lending him his plane for a year; for the same reason, he will do no harm to a second, a third, a fourth borrower, in the subsequent periods. Hence you may understand that the interest of a capital is as natural, as lawful, as useful, in the thousandth year, as in the first. We may go still further. It may happen that James lends more than a single plane. It is possible, that by means of working, of saving, of privations, of order, of activity, he may come to lend a multitude of planes and saws; that is to say, to do a multitude of services. I insist upon this point,—that if the first loan has been a social good, it will be the same with all the others; for they are all similar, and based upon the same principle. It may happen, then, that the amount of all the remunerations received by our honest operative, in exchange for services rendered by him, may suffice to maintain him. In this case, there will be a man in the world who has a right to live without working. I do not say that he would be doing right to give himself up to idleness—but I say, that he has a right to do so; and if he does so, it will be at nobody's expense, but quite the contrary. If society at all understands the nature of things, it will acknowledge that this man subsists on services which he receives certainly (as we all do), but which he lawfully receives in exchange for other services, which he himself has rendered, that he continues to render, and which are quite real, inasmuch as they are freely and voluntarily accepted.

And here we have a glimpse of one of the finest harmonies in the social world. I allude to *leisure:* not that leisure that the warlike and tyrannical classes arrange for themselves by the plunder of the workers, but that leisure which is the lawful and innocent fruit of past activity and economy. In expressing myself thus, I know that I shall shock many received ideas. But see! Is not leisure an essential spring in the social machine? Without it, the world would never have had a Newton, a Pascal, a Fenelon; mankind would have been ignorant of all arts, sciences, and of those wonderful inventions prepared originally by investigations of mere curiosity; thought would have been inert—man would have made no progress. On the other hand, if leisure could only be explained by plunder and oppression—if it were a benefit which could only be enjoyed unjustly, and at the expense of others, there would be no middle path between these two evils; either mankind would be reduced to the necessity of stagnating in a vegetable and stationary life, in eternal ignorance, from the absence of wheels to its machine—or else it would have to acquire these wheels at the price of inevitable injustice, and would necessarily present the sad spectacle, in one form or other, of the antique classification of human beings into masters and slaves. I defy any one to show me, in this case, any other alternative. We should be compelled to contemplate the Divine plan which governs society, with the regret of thinking that it presents a deplorable chasm. The stimulus of progress would be forgotten, or, which is worse, this stimulus would be no other than injustice itself. But no! God has not left such a chasm in His work of love. We must take care not to disregard His wisdom and power; for those whose imperfect meditations cannot explain the lawfulness of leisure, are very much like the astronomer who said, at a certain point in the heavens there ought to exist a planet which will be at last discovered, for without it the celestial world is not harmony, but discord.

Well, I say that, if well understood, the history of my humble plane, although very modest, is sufficient to raise us to the contemplation of one of the most consoling, but least understood of the social harmonies.

It is not true that we must choose between the denial or the unlawfulness of leisure; thanks to rent and its natural duration, leisure may arise from labour and saving. It is a pleasing prospect, which every one may have in view; a noble recompense, to which each may aspire. It makes its appearance in the world; it distributes itself proportionably to the exercise of certain virtues; it opens all the avenues to intelligence; it ennobles, it raises the morals; it spiritualizes the soul of humanity, not only without laying any weight on those of our brethren whose lot in life devotes them to severe labour, but relieving them gradually from the heaviest and most repugnant part of this labour. It is enough that capitals should be formed, accumulated, multiplied; should be lent on conditions less and less burdensome; that they should descend, penetrate into every social circle, and that by an admirable progression, after having liberated the lenders, they should hasten the liberation of the borrowers themselves. For that end, the laws and customs ought all to be favourable to economy, the source of capital. It is enough to say, that the first of all these conditions is, not to alarm, to attack, to deny that which is the stimulus of saving and the reason of its existence—interest.

As long as we see nothing passing from hand to hand, in the character of loan, but *provisions, materials, instruments,* things indispensable to the productiveness of labour itself, the ideas thus far exhibited will not find many opponents. Who knows, even, that I may not be reproached for having made a great effort to burst what may be said to be an open door. But as soon as *cash* makes its appearance as the subject of the transaction (and it is this which appears almost always), immediately a crowd of objections are raised. Money, it will be said, will not reproduce it self, like your *sack of corn;* it does not assist labour, like your *plane;* it does not afford an immediate satisfaction, like your *house.* It is incapable, by its nature, of producing interest, of multiplying itself, and the remuneration it demands is a positive extortion.

Who cannot see the sophistry of this? Who does not see that cash is only a transient form, which men give at the time to other *values,* to real objects of usefulness, for the sole object of facilitating their arrangements? In the midst of social complications, the man who is in a condition to lend, scarcely ever has the exact thing which the borrower wants. James, it is true, has a plane; but, perhaps, William wants a saw. They cannot negotiate; the transaction favourable to both cannot take place, and then what happens? It happens that James first exchanges his plane for money; he lends the money to William, and William exchanges the money for a saw. The transaction is no longer a simple one; it is decomposed into two parts, as I explained above in speaking of exchange. But, for all that, it has not changed its nature; it still contains all the elements of a direct loan. James has still got rid of a tool which was useful to him; William has still received an instrument which perfects his work and increases his profits; there is still a service rendered by the lender, which entitles him to receive an equivalent service from the borrower; this just balance is not the less established by free mutual bargaining. The very natural obligation to restore at the end of the term the entire *value,* still constitutes the principle of the duration of interest.

At the end of a year, says M. Thore, will you find an additional crown in a bag of a hundred pounds?

No, certainly, if the borrower puts the bag of one hundred pounds on the shelf. In such a case, neither the plane nor the sack of corn would reproduce themselves. But it is not for the sake of leaving the money in the bag, nor the plane on the hook, that they are borrowed. The plane is borrowed to be used, or the money to procure a plane. And if it is clearly proved that this tool enables the borrower to obtain profits which he would not have made without it, if it is proved that the lender has renounced creating for himself this excess of profits, we may understand how the stipulation of a part of this excess of profits in favour of the lender, is equitable and lawful.

Ignorance of the true part which cash plays in human transactions, is the source of the most fatal errors. I intend devoting an entire pamphlet to this subject. From what we may infer from the writings of M. Proudhon, that which has led him to think that gratuitous credit was a logical and definite consequence of social progress, is the observation of the phenomenon which shows a decreasing interest, almost in direct proportion to the rate of civilisation. In barbarous times it is, in fact, cent, per cent., and more. Then it descends to eighty, sixty, fifty, forty, twenty, ten, eight, five, four, and three per cent. In Holland, it has even been as low as two per cent. Hence it is concluded, that "in proportion as society comes to perfection, it will descend to zero by the time civilisation is complete. In other words, that which characterises social perfection is the gratuitousness of credit. When, therefore, we shall have abolished interest, we shall have reached the last step of progress." This is mere sophistry, and as such false arguing may contribute to render popular the unjust, dangerous, and destructive dogma, that credit should be gratuitous, by representing it as coincident with social perfection, with the reader's permission I will examine in a few words this new view of the question.

What is *interest?* It is the service rendered, after a free bargain, by the borrower to the lender, in remuneration for the service he has received by the loan. By what law is the rate of these remunerative services established? By the general law which regulates the equivalent of all services; that is, by the law of supply and demand.

The more easily a thing is procured, the smaller is the service rendered by yielding it or lending it. The man who gives me a glass of water in the Pyrenees, does not render me so great a service as he who allows me one in the desert of Sahara. If there are many planes, sacks of corn, or houses, in a country, the use of them is obtained, other things being equal, on more favourable conditions than if they were few; for the simple reason, that the lender renders in this case a smaller *relative service.*

It is not surprising, therefore, that the more abundant capitals are, the lower is the interest.

Is this saying that it will ever reach zero? No; because, I repeat it, the principle of a remuneration is in the loan. To say that interest will be annihilated, is to say that there will never be any motive for saving, for denying ourselves, in order to form new capitals, nor even to preserve the old ones. In this case, the waste would immediately bring a void, and interest would directly reappear.

In that, the nature of the services of which we are speaking does not differ from any other. Thanks to industrial progress, a pair of stockings, which used to be worth six francs, has successively been worth only four, three, and two. No one can say to what point this value will descend; but we can affirm that it will never reach zero, unless the stockings finish by producing themselves spontaneously. Why? Because the principle of remuneration is in labour; because he who works for another renders a service, and ought to receive a service. If no one paid for stockings, they would cease to be made; and, with the scarcity, the price would not fail to reappear.

The sophism which I am now combating has its root in the infinite divisibility which belongs to *value,* as it does to matter.

It appears at first paradoxical, but it is well known to all mathematicians, that, through all eternity, fractions may be taken from a weight without the weight ever being annihilated. It is sufficient that each successive fraction be less than the preceding one, in a determined and regular proportion.

There are countries where people apply themselves to increasing the size of horses, or diminishing in sheep the size of the head. It is impossible to say precisely to what point they will arrive in this. No one can say that he has seen the largest horse or the smallest sheep's head that will ever appear in the world. But he may safely say that the size of horses will never attain to infinity, nor the heads of sheep to nothing.

The arguments of M. Proudhon reduce themselves, then, to this:—Since the most skilful agriculturists are those who have reduced the heads of sheep to the smallest size, we shall have arrived at the highest agricultural perfection when sheep have no longer any heads. Therefore, in order to realise the perfection, let us behead them.In the same way, no one can say to what point the price of stockings nor the interest of capitals will come down; but we may safely affirm, when we know the nature of things, that neither the one nor the other will ever arrive at zero, for labour and capital can no more live without recompense than a sheep without a head.

I have now done with this wearisome discussion. Why is it that the breath of false doctrine has made it needful to examine into the intimate nature of interest? I must not leave off without remarking upon a beautiful moral which may be drawn from this law:—"The depression of interest is proportioned to the abundance of capitals." This law being granted, if there is a class of men to whom it is more important than to any other that capitals be formed, accumulate, multiply, abound, and superabound, it is certainly the class which borrows them directly or indirectly; it is those men who operate upon *materials,* who gain assistance by *instruments,* who live upon *provisions,* produced and economised by other men.

Imagine, in a vast and fertile country, a population of a thousand inhabitants, destitute of all capital thus defined. It will assuredly perish by the pangs of hunger. Let us suppose a case hardly less cruel. Let us suppose that ten of these savages are provided with instruments and provisions sufficient to work and to live themselves until harvest time, as well as to remunerate the services of eighty labourers. The inevitable result will be the death of nine hundred human beings. It is clear, then, that since 990 men, urged by want, will crowd upon the supports which would only maintain a hundred, the ten capitalists will be masters of the market. They will obtain labour on the hardest conditions, for they will put it up to auction, or the highest bidder. And observe this,—if these capitalists entertain such pious sentiments as would induce them to impose personal privations on themselves, in order to diminish the sufferings of some of their brethren, this generosity, which attaches to morality, will be as noble in its principle as useful in its effects. But if, duped by that false philosophy which persons wish so inconsiderately to mingle with economic laws, they take to remunerating labour largely, far from doing good, they will do harm. They will give double wages, it may be. But then, forty-five men will be better provided for, whilst forty-five others will come to augment the number of those who are sinking into the grave. Upon this supposition, it is not the lowering of wages which is the mischief, it is the scarcity of capital. Low wages are not the cause, but the effect of the evil. I may add, that they are to a certain extent the remedy. It acts in this way: it distributes the burden of suffering as much as it can, and saves as many lives as a limited quantity of sustenance permits.

Suppose now, that instead of ten capitalists, there should be a hundred, two hundred, five hundred,—is it not evident that the condition of the whole population, and, above all, that of the "proletaires,"[1] will be more and more improved? Is it not evident that, apart from every consideration of generosity, they would obtain more work and better pay for it?—that

1. Common people.

they themselves will be in a better condition, to form capitals, without being able to fix the limits to this ever-increasing facility of realising equality and well-being? Would it not be madness in them to admit such doctrines, and to act in a way which would drain the source of wages, and paralyse the activity and stimulus of saving? Let them learn this lesson, then; doubtless, capitals are good for those who possess them: who denies it? But they are also useful to those who have not yet been able to form them; and it is important to those who have them not, that others should have them.

Yes, if the "proletaires" knew their true interests, they would seek, with the greatest care, what circumstances are, and what are not favourable to saving, in order to favour the former and to discourage the latter. They would sympathise with every measure which tends to the rapid formation of capitals. They would be enthusiastic promoters of peace, liberty, order, security, the union of classes and peoples, economy, moderation in public expenses, simplicity in the machinery of government; for it is under the sway of all these circumstances that saving does its work, brings plenty within the reach of the masses, invites those persons to become the formers of capital who were formerly under the necessity of borrowing upon hard conditions. They would repel with energy the warlike spirit, which diverts from its true course so large a part of human labour; the monopolising spirit, which deranges the equitable distribution of riches, in the way by which liberty alone can realise it; the multitude of public services, which attack our purses only to check our liberty; and, in short, those subversive, hateful, thoughtless doctrines, which alarm capital, prevent its formation, oblige it to flee, and finally to raise its price, to the especial disadvantage of the workers, who bring it into operation. Well, and in this respect is not the revolution of February a hard lesson? Is it not evident that the insecurity it has thrown into the world of business on the one hand; and, on the other, the advancement of the fatal theories to which I have alluded, and which, from the clubs, have almost penetrated into the regions of the legislature, have everywhere raised the rate of interest? Is it not evident, that from that time the "proletaires" have found greater difficulty in procuring those materials, instruments, and provisions, without which labour is impossible? Is it not that which has caused stoppages; and do not stoppages, in their turn, lower wages? Thus there is a deficiency of labour to the "proletaires," from the same cause which loads the objects they consume with an increase of price, in consequence of the rise of interest. High interest, low wages, means in other words that the same article preserves its price, but that the part of the capitalist has invaded, without profiting himself, that of the workmen.

A friend of mine, commissioned to make inquiry into Parisian industry, has assured me that the manufacturers have revealed to him a very striking fact, which proves, better than any reasoning can, how much insecurity and uncertainty injure the formation of capital. It was remarked, that during the most distressing period, the popular expenses of mere fancy had not diminished. The small theatres, the fighting lists, the public-houses, and tobacco depots, were as much frequented as in prosperous times. In the inquiry, the operatives themselves explained this phenomenon thus:—"What is the use of pinching? Who knows what will happen to us? Who knows that interest will not be abolished? Who knows but that the State will become a universal and gratuitous lender, and that it will wish to annihilate all the fruits which we might expect from our savings?" Well! I say, that if such ideas could prevail during two single years, it would be enough to turn our beautiful France into a Turkey—misery would become general and endemic, and, most assuredly, the poor would be the first upon whom it would fall.

Workmen! they talk to you a great deal upon the *artificial* organisation of labour;—do you know why they do so? Because they are ignorant of the laws of its *natural* organisation; that is, of the wonderful organisation which results from liberty. You are told, that liberty gives rise to what is called the radical antagonism of classes; that it creates, and makes to clash, two opposite interests—that of the capitalists and that of the "proletaires." But we ought to begin by proving that this antagonism exists by a law of nature; and afterwards it would remain to be shown how far the arrangements of restraint are superior to those of liberty, for between liberty and restraint I see no middle path. Again, it would remain to be proved that restraint would always operate to your advantage, and to the prejudice of the rich. But, no; this radical antagonism, this natural opposition of interests, does not exist. It is only an evil dream of perverted and intoxicated imaginations. No; a plan so defective has not proceeded from the Divine Mind. To affirm it, we must begin by denying the existence of

God. And see how, by means of social laws, and because men exchange amongst themselves their labours and their productions, see what a harmonious tie attaches the classes one to the other! There are the landowners; what is their interest? That the soil be fertile, and the sun beneficent: and what is the result? That corn abounds, that it falls in price, and the advantage turns to the profit of those who have had no patrimony. There are the manufacturers—what is their constant thought? To perfect their labour, to increase the power of their machines, to procure for themselves, upon the best terms, the raw material. And to what does all this tend? To the abundance and the low price of produce; that is, that all the efforts of the manufacturers, and without their suspecting it, result in a profit to the public consumer, of which each of you is one. It is the same with every profession. Well, the capitalists are not exempt from this law. They are very busy making schemes, economising, and turning them to their advantage. This is all very well; but the more they succeed, the more do they promote the abundance of capital, and, as a necessary consequence, the reduction of interest. Now, who is it that profits by the reduction of interest? Is it not the borrower first, and finally, the consumers of the things which the capitals contribute to produce?

It is therefore certain that the final result of the efforts of each class is the common good of all.

You are told that capital tyrannises over labour. I do not deny that each one endeavours to draw the greatest possible advantage from his situation; but, in this sense, he realises only that which is possible. Now, it is never more possible for capitals to tyrannise over labour, than when they are scarce; for then it is they who make the law—it is they who regulate the rate of sale. Never is this tyranny more impossible to them, than when they are abundant; for, in that case, it is labour which has the command.

Away, then, with the jealousies of classes, ill-will, unfounded hatreds, unjust suspicions. These depraved passions injure those who nourish them in their hearts. This is no declamatory morality; it is a chain of causes and effects, which is capable of being rigorously, mathematically demonstrated. It is not the less sublime, in that it satisfies the intellect as well as the feelings.

I shall sum up this whole dissertation with these words:—Workmen, labourers, "proletaires," destitute and suffering classes, will you improve your condition? You will not succeed by strife, insurrection, hatred, and error. But there are three things which cannot perfect the entire community, without extending these benefits to yourselves; these things are—peace, liberty, and security.

WHAT IS MONEY?

"Hateful money! hateful money!" cried F——, the economist, despairingly, as he came from the Committee of Finance, where a project of paper money had just been discussed.

"What's the matter?" said I. "What is the meaning of this sudden dislike to the most extolled of all the divinities of this world?"

F——: Hateful money! hateful money!

Bastiat: You alarm me. I hear peace, liberty, and life cried down, and Brutus went so far even as to say, "Virtue! thou art but a name!" But what can have happened?

F: Hateful money! hateful money!

B: Come, come, exercise a little philosophy. What has happened to you? Has Croesus been affecting you? Has Mondor been playing you false? or has Zoilus been libelling you in the papers?

F: I have nothing to do with Croesus; my character, by its insignificance, is safe from any slanders of Zoilus; and as to Mondor—

B: Ah! now I have it. How could I be so blind? You, too, are the inventor of a social reorganization—of the *F——system,* in fact. Your society is to be more perfect than that of Sparta, and, therefore, all money is to be rigidly banished from it. And the thing that troubles you is, how to persuade your people to empty their purses. What would you have? This is the rock on which all reorganizers split. There is not one, but would do wonders, if he could only contrive to overcome all resisting influences, and if all mankind would consent to become soft wax in his fingers; but men are resolved not to be soft wax; they listen, applaud, or reject, and—go on as before.

F: Thank heaven, I am still free from this fashionable mania. Instead of inventing social laws, I am studying those which it has pleased Providence to invent, and I am delighted to find them admirable in their progressive development. This is why I exclaim, "Hateful money! hateful money!"

B: You are a disciple of Proudhon, then? Well, there is a very simple way for you to satisfy yourself. Throw your purse into the Seine, only reserving a hundred sous, to take an action from the Bank of Exchange.

F: If I cry out against money, is it likely I should tolerate its deceitful substitute?

B: Then I have only one more guess to make. You are a new Diogenes, and are going to victimize me with a discourse *a la Seneca,* on the contempt of riches.

F: Heaven preserve me from that! For riches, don't you see, are not a little more or a little less money. They are bread for the hungry, clothes for the naked, fuel to warm you, oil to lengthen the day, a career open to your son, a certain portion for your daughter, a day of rest after fatigue, a cordial for the faint, a little assistance slipped into the hand of a poor man, a shelter from the storm, a diversion for a brain worn by thought, the incomparable pleasure of making those happy who are dear to us. Riches are instruction, independence, dignity, confidence, charity; they are progress, and civilization. Riches are the admirable civilizing result of two admirable agents, more civilizing even than riches themselves—labour and exchange.

B: Well! now you seem to be singing the praises of riches, when, a moment ago, you were loading them with imprecations!

F: Why, don't you see that it was only the whim of an economist? I cry out against money, just because everybody confounds it, as you did just now, with riches, and that this confusion is the cause of errors and calamities without number. I cry out against it because its function in society is not understood, and very difficult to explain. I cry out against it, because it jumbles all ideas, causes the means to be taken for the end, the obstacle for the cause, the alpha for the omega; because its presence in the world, though in itself beneficial, has, nevertheless, introduced a fatal notion, a perversion of principles, a contradictory theory, which, in a multitude of forms, has impoverished mankind and deluged the earth with blood. I cry out against it, because I feel that I am incapable of contending against the error to which it has given birth, otherwise than by a long and fastidious dissertation to which no one would listen. Oh! if I could only find a patient and benevolent listener!

B: Well, it shall not be said that for want of a victim you remain in the state of irritation in which you now are. I am listening; speak, lecture, do not restrain yourself in any way.

F: You promise to take an interest?

B: I promise to have patience.

F: That is not much.

B: It is all that I can give. Begin, and explain to me, at first, how a mistake on the subject of cash, if mistake there be, is to be found at the root of all economical errors?

F: Well, now, is it possible that you can conscientiously assure me, that you have never happened to confound wealth with money?

B: I don't know; but, after all, what would be the consequence of such a confusion?

F: Nothing very important. An error in your brain, which would have no influence over your actions; for you see that, with respect to labour and exchange, although there are as many opinions as there are heads, we all act in the same way.

B: Just as we walk upon the same principle, although we are not agreed upon the theory of equilibrium and gravitation.

F: Precisely. A person who argued himself into the opinion that during the night our heads and feet changed places, might write very fine books upon the subject, but still he would walk about like everybody else.

B: So I think. Nevertheless, he would soon suffer the penalty of being too much of a logician.

F: In the same way, a man would die of hunger, who having decided that money is real wealth, should carry out the idea to the end. That is the reason that this theory is false, for there is no true theory but such as results from facts themselves, as manifested at all times, and in all places.

B: I can understand, that practically, and under the influence of personal interest, the fatal effects of the erroneous action would tend to correct an error. But if that of which you speak has so little influence, why does it disturb you so much?

F: Because, when a man, instead of acting for himself, decides for others, personal interest, that ever watchful and sensible sentinel, is no longer present to cry out, "Stop! the responsibility is misplaced." It is Peter who is deceived, and John suffers; the false system of the legislator necessarily becomes the rule of action of whole populations. And observe the difference. When you have money, and are very hungry, whatever your theory on cash may be, what do you do?

B: I go to a baker's, and buy some bread.

F: You do not hesitate about getting rid of your money?

B: The only use of money is to buy what one wants.

F: And if the baker should happen to be thirsty, what does he do?

B: He goes to the wine merchant's, and buys wine with the money I have given him.

F: What! is he not afraid he shall ruin himself?

B: The real ruin would be to go without eating or drinking.

F: And everybody in the world, if he is free, acts in the same manner?

B: Without a doubt. Would you have them die of hunger for the sake of laying by pence?

F: So far from it, that I consider they act wisely, and I only wish that the theory was nothing but the faithful image of this universal practice. But, suppose now that you were the legislator, the absolute king of a vast empire, where there were no gold mines.

B: No unpleasant fiction.

F: Suppose, again, that you were perfectly convinced of this,—that wealth consists solely and exclusively in cash; to what conclusion would you come?

B: I should conclude that there was no other means for me to enrich my people, or for them to enrich themselves, but to draw away the cash from other nations.

F: That is to say, to impoverish them. The first conclusion, then, to which you would arrive would be this,—a nation can only gain when another loses.

B: This axiom has the authority of Bacon and Montaigne.

F: It is not the less sorrowful for that, for it implies—that progress is impossible. Two nations, no more than two men, cannot prosper side by side.

B: It would seem that such is the result of this principle.

F: And as all men are ambitious to enrich themselves, it follows that all are desirous, according to a law of Providence, of ruining their fellow-creatures.

B: This is not Christianity, but it is political economy.

F: Such a doctrine is detestable. But, to continue, I have made you an absolute king. You must not be satisfied with reasoning, you must act. There is no limit to your power. How would you treat this doctrine,—wealth is money?

B: It would be my endeavour to increase, incessantly, among my people the quantity of cash.

F: But there are no mines in your kingdom. How would you set about it? What would you do?

B: I should do nothing: I should merely forbid, on pain of death, that a single crown should leave the country.

F: And if your people should happen to be hungry as well as rich?

F: So that, by your own confession, you would force them to act upon a principle equally opposite to that upon which you would yourself act under similar circumstances. Why so?**B:** Never mind. In the system we are discussing, to allow them to export crowns would be to allow them to impoverish themselves.

B: Just because my own hunger touches me, and the hunger of a nation does not touch legislators.

F: Well, I can tell you that your plan would fail, and that no superintendence would be sufficiently vigilant, when the people were hungry, to prevent the crowns from going out and the corn from coming in.

B: If so, this plan, whether erroneous or not, would effect nothing; it would do neither good nor harm, and therefore requires no further consideration.

F: You forget that you are a legislator. A legislator must not be disheartened at trifles, when he is making experiments on others. The first measure not having succeeded, you ought to take some other means of attaining your end.

B: What end?

F: You must have a bad memory. Why, that of increasing, in the midst of your people, the quantity of cash, which is presumed to be true wealth.

B: Ah! to be sure; I beg your pardon. But then you see, as they say of music, a little is enough; and this may be said, I think, with still more reason, of political economy. I must consider. But really I don't know how to contrive—

F: Ponder it well. First, I would have you observe that your first plan solved the problem only negatively. To prevent the crowns from going out of the country is the way to prevent the wealth from diminishing, but it is not the way to increase it.

B: Ah! now I am beginning to see . . . the corn which is allowed to come in . . . a bright idea strikes me . . . the contrivance is ingenious, the means infallible; I am coming to it now.

F: Now, I, in turn, must ask you—to what?

B: Why, to a means of increasing the quantity of cash.

F: How would you set about it, if you please?

B: Is it not evident that if the heap of money is to be constantly increasing, the first condition is that none must be taken from it?

F: Certainly.

B: And the second, that additions must constantly be made to it?

F. To be sure.

B: Then the problem will be solved, either negatively or positively, as the Socialists say, if on the one hand I prevent the foreigner from taking from it, and on the other I oblige him to add to it.

F: Better and better.

B: And for this there must be two simple laws made, in which cash will not even be mentioned. By the one, my subjects will be forbidden to buy anything abroad; and by the other, they will be required to sell a great deal.

F: A well-advised plan.

B: Is it new? I must take out a patent for the invention.

F: You need do no such thing; you have been forestalled. But you must take care of one thing.

B: What is that?

F: I have made you an absolute king. I understand that you are going to prevent your subjects from buying foreign productions. It will be enough if you prevent them from entering the country. Thirty or forty thousand custom-house officers will do the business.

B: It would be rather expensive. But what does that signify? The money they receive will not go out of the country.

F: True; and in this system it is the grand point. But to ensure a sale abroad, how would you proceed?

B: I should encourage it by prizes, obtained by means of some good taxes laid upon my people.

F: In this case, the exporters, constrained by competition among themselves, would lower their prices in proportion, and it would be like making a present to the foreigner of the prizes or of the taxes.

B: Still, the money would not go out of the country.

F: Of course. That is understood. But if your system is beneficial, the kings around you will adopt it. They will make similar plans to yours; they will have their custom-house officers, and reject your productions; so that with them, as with you, the heap of money may not be diminished.

B: I shall have an army and force their barriers.

F: They will have an army and force yours.

B: I shall arm vessels, make conquests, acquire colonies, and create consumers for my people, who will be obliged to eat our corn and drink our wine.

F: The other kings will do the same. They will dispute your conquests, your colonies, and your consumers; then on all sides there will be war, and all will be uproar.

B: I shall raise my taxes, and increase my custom-house officers, my army, and my navy.

F: The others will do the same.

B: I shall redouble my exertions.

F: The others will redouble theirs. In the meantime, we have no proof that you would succeed in selling to a great extent.

B: It is but too true. It would be well if the commercial efforts would neutralize each other.

F: And the military efforts also. And, tell me, are not these custom-house officers, soldiers, and vessels, these oppressive taxes, this perpetual struggle towards an impossible result, this permanent state of open or secret war with the whole world, are they not the logical and inevitable consequence of the legislators having adopted an idea, which you admit is acted upon by no man who is his own master, that "wealth is cash; and to increase cash, is to increase wealth?"

B: I grant it. Either the axiom is true, and then the legislator ought to act as I have described, although universal war should be the consequence; or it is false; and in this case men, in destroying each other, only ruin themselves.

F: And, remember, that before you became a king, this same axiom had led you by a logical process to the following maxims:—That which one gains, another loses. The profit of one, is the loss of the other:—which maxims imply an unavoidable antagonism amongst all men.

B: It is only too certain. Whether I am a philosopher or a legislator, whether I reason or act upon the principle that money is wealth, I always arrive at one conclusion, or one result:—universal war. It is well that you pointed out the consequences before beginning a discussion upon it; otherwise, I should never have had the courage to follow you to the end of your economical dissertation, for, to tell you the truth, it is not much to my taste.

F: What do you mean? I was just thinking of it when you heard me grumbling against money! I was lamenting that my countrymen have not the courage to study what it is so important that they should know.

B: And yet the consequences are frightful.

F: The consequences! As yet I have only mentioned one. I might have told you of others still more fatal.

B: Yon make my hair stand on end! What other evils can have been caused to mankind by this confusion between money and wealth?

F: It would take me a long time to enumerate them. This doctrine is one of a very numerous family. The eldest, whose acquaintance we have just made, is called the *prohibitive system;* the next, the *colonial system;* the third, *hatred of capital;* the Benjamin, *paper money.*

B: What! does paper money proceed from the same error?

F: Yes, directly. When legislators, after having ruined men by war and taxes, persevere in their idea, they say to themselves, "If the people suffer, it is because there is not money enough. We must make some." And as it is not easy to multiply the precious metals, especially when the pretended resources of prohibition have been exhausted, they add, "We will make fictitious money, nothing is more easy, and then every citizen will have his pocket-book full of it, and they will all be rich."

B: In fact, this proceeding is more expeditious than the other, and then it does not lead to foreign war.

F: No, but it leads to civil war.

B: You are a grumbler. Make haste and dive to the bottom of the question. I am quite impatient, for the first time, to know if money (or its sign) is wealth.

F: You will grant that men do not satisfy any of their wants immediately with crown pieces. If they are hungry, they want bread; if naked, clothing; if they are ill, they must have remedies; if they are cold, they want shelter and fuel; if they would learn, they must have books; if they would travel, they must have conveyances—and so on. The riches of a country consist in the abundance and proper distribution of all these things. Hence you may perceive and rejoice at the falseness of this gloomy maxim of Bacon's, "*What one people gains, another necessarily loses:*" a maxim expressed in a still more discouraging manner by Montaigne, in these words: "*The profit of one is the loss of another.*" When Shem, Ham, and Japhet divided amongst themselves the vast solitudes of this earth, they surely might each of them build, drain, sow, reap, and obtain improved lodging, food and clothing, and better instruction, perfect and enrich themselves—in short, increase their enjoyments, without causing a necessary diminution in the corresponding enjoyments of their brothers. It is the same with two nations.

B: There is no doubt that two nations, the same as two men, unconnected with each other, may, by working more, and working better, prosper at the same time, without injuring each other. It is not this which is denied by the axioms of Montaigne and Bacon. They only mean to say, that in the transactions which take place between two nations or two men, if one gains, the other must lose. And this is self-evident, as exchange adds nothing by itself to the mass of those useful things of which you were speaking; for if, after the exchange, one of the parties is found to have gained something, the other will, of course, be found to have lost something.

F: You have formed a very incomplete, nay a false idea of exchange. If Shem is located upon a plain which is fertile in corn, Japhet upon a slope adapted for growing the vine, Ham upon a rich pasturage,—the distinction of their occupations, far from hurting any of them, might cause all three to prosper more. It must be so, in fact, for the distribution of labour, introduced by exchange, will have the effect of increasing the mass of corn, wine, and meat, which is produced, and which is to be shared. How can it be otherwise, if you allow liberty in these transactions? From the moment that any one of the brothers should perceive that labour in company, as it were, was a permanent loss, compared to solitary labour, he would cease to exchange. Exchange brings with it its claim to our gratitude. The fact of its being accomplished, proves that it is a good thing.

B: But Bacon's axiom is true in the case of gold and silver. If we admit that at a certain moment there exists in the world a given quantity, it is perfectly clear that one purse cannot be filled without another being emptied.

F: And if gold is considered to be riches, the natural conclusion is, that displacements of fortune take place among men, but no general progress. It is just what I said when I began. If, on the contrary, you look upon an abundance of useful things, fit for satisfying our wants and our tastes, as true riches, you will see that simultaneous prosperity is possible. Cash serves only to facilitate the transmission of these useful things from one to another, which may be done equally well with an ounce of rare metal like gold, with a pound of more abundant material as silver, or with a hundred-weight of still more abundant metal, as copper. According to that, if the French had at their disposal as much again of all these useful things, France would be twice as rich, although the quantity of cash remained the same; but it would not be the same if there were double the cash, for in that case the amount of useful things would not increase.

B: The question to be decided is, whether the presence of a greater number of crowns has not the effect, precisely, of augmenting the sum of useful things?

F: What connexion can there be between these two terms? Food, clothing, houses, fuel, all come from nature and from labour, from more or less skilful labour exerted upon a more or less liberal nature.

B: You are forgetting one great force, which is—exchange. If you acknowledge that this is a force, as you have admitted that crowns facilitate it, you must also allow that they have an indirect power of production.

F: But I have added, that a small quantity of rare metal facilitates transactions as much as a large quantity of abundant metal; whence it follows, that a people is not enriched by being *forced* to give up useful things for the sake of having more money.

B: Thus, it is your opinion that the treasures discovered in California will not increase the wealth of the world?

F: I do not believe that, on the whole, they will add much to the enjoyments, to the real satisfactions of mankind. If the Californian gold merely replaces in the world that which has been lost and destroyed, it may have its use. If it increases the amount of cash, it will depreciate it. The gold diggers will be richer than they would have been without it. But those in whose possession the gold is at the moment of its depreciation, will obtain a smaller gratification for the same amount. I cannot look upon this as an increase, but as a displacement of true riches, as I have defined them.

B: All that is very plausible. But you will not easily convince me that I am not richer (all other things being equal) if I have two crowns, than if I had only one.

F: I do not deny it.

B: And what is true of me is true of my neighbour, and of the neighbour of my neighbour, and so on, from one to another, all over the country. Therefore, if every Frenchman has more crowns, France must be more rich.

F: And here you fall into the common mistake of concluding that what affects one affects all, and thus confusing the individual with the general interest.

B: Why, what can be more conclusive? What is true of one, must be so of all! What are all, but a collection of individuals? You might as well tell me that every Frenchman could suddenly grow an inch taller, without the average height of Frenchmen being increased.

F: Your reasoning is apparently sound, I grant you, and that is why the illusion it conceals is so common. However, let us examine it a little. Ten persons were at play. For greater ease, they had adopted the plan of each taking ten counters, and against these they had placed a hundred francs under a candlestick, so that each counter corresponded to ten francs. After the game the winnings were adjusted, and the players drew from the candlestick as many ten francs as would represent the number of counters. Seeing this, one of them, a great arithmetician perhaps, but an indifferent reasoner, said—"Gentlemen, experience invariably teaches me that, at the end of the game, I find myself a gainer in proportion to the number of my counters. Have you not observed the same with regard to yourselves? Thus, what is true of me must be true of each of you, and *what is true of each must be true of all.* We should, therefore, all of us gain more, at the end of the game, if we all had more counters. Now, nothing can be easier; we have only to distribute twice the number." This was done; but when the game was finished, and they came to adjust the winnings, it was found that the thousand francs under the candlestick had not been miraculously multiplied, according to the general expectation. They had to be divided accordingly, and the only result obtained (chimerical enough) was this;—every one had, it is true, his double number of counters, but every counter, instead of corresponding to *ten* francs, only represented *five.* Thus it was clearly shown, that what is true of each, is not always true of all.

B: I see; you are supposing a general increase of counters, without a corresponding increase of the sum placed under the candlestick.

F: And you are supposing a general increase of crowns, without a corresponding increase of things, the exchange of which is facilitated by these crowns.

B: Do you compare the crowns to counters?

F: In any other point of view, certainly not; but in the case you place before me, and which I have to argue against, I do. Remark one thing. In order that there be a general increase of crowns in a country, this country must have mines, or its commerce must be such as to give useful things in exchange for cash. Apart from these two circumstances, a universal increase is impossible, the crowns only changing hands; and in this case, although it may be very true that each one, taken individually, is richer in proportion to the number of crowns that he has, we cannot draw the inference which you drew just now, because a crown more in one purse implies necessarily a crown less in some other. It is the same as with your comparison of the middle height. If each of us grew only at the expense of others, it would be very true of each, taken individually, that he would be a taller man if he had the chance, but this would never be true of the whole taken collectively.

B: Be it so: but, in the two suppositions that you have made, the increase is real, and you must allow that I am right.

F: To a certain point, gold and silver have a value. To obtain this, men consent to give useful things which have a value also. When, therefore, there are mines in a country, if that country obtains from them sufficient gold to purchase a useful thing from abroad—a locomotive, for instance—it enriches itself with all the enjoyments which a locomotive can procure, exactly as if the machine had been made at home. The question is, whether it spends more efforts in the former proceeding than in the latter? For if it did not export this gold, it would depreciate, and something worse would happen than what you see in California, for there, at least, the precious metals are used to buy useful things made elsewhere. Nevertheless, there is still a danger that they may starve on heaps of gold. What would it be if the law prohibited exportation? As to the second supposition—that of the gold which we obtain by trade; it is an advantage, or the reverse, according as the country stands more or less in need of it, compared to its wants of the useful things which must be given up in order to obtain it. It is not for the law to judge of this, but for those who are concerned in it; for if the law should start upon this principle, that gold is preferable to useful things, whatever may be their value, and if it should act effectually in this sense, it would tend to make France another California, where there would be a great deal of cash to spend, and nothing to buy. It is the very same system which is represented by Midas.

B: The gold which is imported implies that a *useful thing* is *ex*ported, and in this respect there is a satisfaction withdrawn from the country. But is there not a corresponding benefit? And will not this gold be the source of a number of new satisfactions, by circulating from hand to hand, and inciting to labour and industry, until at length it leaves the country in its turn, and causes the importation of some useful thing?

F: Now you have come to the heart of the question. Is it true that a crown is the principle which causes the production of all the objects whose exchange it facilitates? It is very clear that a piece of five francs is only *worth* five francs; but we are led to believe that this value has a particular character: that it is not consumed like other things, or that it is exhausted very gradually; that it renews itself, as it were, in each transaction; and that, finally this crown has been worth five francs, as many times as it has accomplished transactions—that it is of itself worth all the things for which it has been successively exchanged; and this is believed, because it is supposed that without this crown these things would never have been produced. It is said, the shoemaker would have sold fewer shoes, consequently he would have bought less of the butcher; the butcher would not have gone so often to the grocer, the grocer to the doctor, the doctor to the lawyer, and so on.

B: No one can dispute that.

B: But if we all had a great number of crowns we should obtain from society many services. Would not that be very desirable?**F:** This is the time, then, to analyse the true function of cash, independently of mines and importations. You have a crown. What does it imply in your hands? It is, as it were, the witness and proof that you have, at some time or other, performed some labour, which, instead of profiting by it, you have bestowed upon society in the person of your client. This crown testifies that you have performed a *service* for society, and, moreover, it shows the value of it. It bears witness, besides, that you have not yet obtained from society a *real* equivalent service, to which you have a right. To place you in a condition to exercise this right, at the time and in the manner you please, society, by means of your client, has given you an acknowledgment, a title, a privilege from the republic, a counter, a crown in fact, which only differs from executive titles by bearing its value in itself; and if you are able to read with your mind's eye the inscriptions stamped upon it you will distinctly decipher these words:—"*Pay the bearer a service equivalent to what he has rendered to society, the value received being shown, proved, and measured by that which is represented by me.*" Now, you give up your crown to me. Either my title to it is gratuitous, or it is a claim. If you give it me as payment for a service, the following is the result:—your account with society for real satisfactions is regulated, balanced, and closed. You had rendered it a service for a crown, you now restore the crown for a service; as far as you are concerned, you are clear. As for me, I am just in the position in which you were just now. It is I who am now in advance to society for the service which I have just rendered it in your person. I am become its creditor for the value of the labour which I have performed for you, and which I might devote to myself. It is into my hands, then, that the title of this credit—the proof of this social debt—ought to pass. You cannot say that I am any richer; if I am entitled to receive, it is because I have given. Still less can you say that society is a crown richer, because one of its members has a crown more, and another has one less. For if you let me have this crown gratis, it is certain that I shall be so much the richer, but you will be so much the poorer for it; and the social fortune, taken in a mass, will have undergone no change, because as I have already said, this fortune consists in real services, in effective satisfactions, in useful things. You were a creditor to society, you made me a substitute to your rights, and it signifies little to society, which owes a service, whether it pays the debt to you or to me. This is discharged as soon as the bearer of the claim is paid.

F: You forget that in the process which I have described, and which is a picture of the reality, we only obtain services from society because we have bestowed some upon it. Whoever speaks of a *service,* speaks at the same time of a service *received* and *returned,* for these two terms imply each other, so that the one must always be balanced by the other. It is impossible for society to render more services than it receives, and yet this is the chimera which is being pursued by means of the multiplication of coins, of paper money, &c.

B: All that appears very reasonable in theory, but in practice I cannot help thinking, when I see how things go, that if, by some fortunate circumstance, the number of crowns could be multiplied in such a way that each of us could see his little property doubled, we should all be more at our ease; we should all make more purchases, and trade would receive a powerful stimulus.

F: More purchases! and what should we buy? Doubtless, useful articles—things likely to procure for us substantial gratification—such as provisions, stuffs, houses, books, pictures. You should begin, then, by proving that all these things create themselves; you must suppose the Mint melting ingots of gold which have fallen from the moon; or that the Board of Assignats be put in action at the national printing office; for you cannot reasonably think that if the quantity of corn, cloth, ships, hats and shoes remains the same, the share of each of us can be greater, because we each go to market with a greater number of real or fictitious money. Remember the players. In the social order, the useful things are what the workers place under the candlestick, and the crowns which circulate from hand to hand are the counters. If you multiply the francs without multiplying the useful things, the only result will be, that more francs will be required for each exchange, just as the players required more counters for each deposit. You have the proof of this in what passes for gold silver, and copper. Why does the same exchange require more copper than silver, more silver than gold? Is it not because these metals are distributed in the world in different proportions? What reason have you to suppose that if gold were suddenly to become as abundant as silver, it would not require as much of one as of the other to buy a house?

B: You may be right, but I should prefer your being wrong. In the midst of the sufferings which surround us, so distressing in themselves, and so dangerous in their consequences, I have found some consolation in thinking that there was an easy method of making all the members of the community happy.

F: Even if gold and silver were true riches, it would be no easy matter to increase the amount of them in a country where there are no mines.

B: No, but it is easy to substitute something else. I agree with you that gold and silver can do but little service, except as a mere means of exchange. It is the same with paper money, bank-notes, &c. Then, if we had all of us plenty of the latter, which it is so easy to create, we might all buy a great deal, and should want for nothing. Your cruel theory dissipates hopes, illusions, if you will, whose principle is assuredly very philanthropic.

F: Yes, like all other barren dreams formed to promote universal felicity. The extreme facility of the means which you recommend is quite sufficient to expose its hollowness. Do you believe that if it were merely needful to print bank-notes in order to satisfy all our wants, our tastes and desires, that mankind would have been contented to go on till now, without having recourse to this plan? I agree with you that the discovery is tempting. It would immediately banish from the world, not only plunder, in its diversified and deplorable forms, but even labour itself, except the Board of Assignats. But we have yet to learn how assignats are to purchase houses, which no one would have built; corn, which no one would have raised; stuffs, which no one would have taken the trouble to weave.

B: One thing strikes me in your argument. You say yourself, that if there is no gain, at any rate there is no loss in multiplying the instrument of exchange, as is seen by the instance of the players, who were quits by a very mild deception. Why, then, refuse the philosopher's stone, which would teach us the secret of changing flints into gold, and, in the meantime, into paper money? Are you so blindly wedded to your logic, that you would refuse to try an experiment where there can be no risk? If you are mistaken, you are depriving the nation, as your numerous adversaries believe, of an immense advantage. If the error is on their side, no harm can result, as you yourself say, beyond the failure of a hope. The measure, excellent in their opinion, in yours is negative. Let it be tried, then, since the worst which can happen is not the realization of an evil, but the non-realization of a benefit.

F: In the first place, the failure of a hope is a very great misfortune to any people. It is also very undesirable that the Government should announce the re-imposition of several taxes on the faith of a resource which must infallibly fail. Nevertheless, your remark would deserve some consideration, if, after the issue of paper money and its depreciation, the equilibrium of values should instantly and simultaneously take place, in all things and in every part of the country. The measure would tend, as in my example of the players, to a universal mystification, upon which the best thing we could do would be to look at one another and laugh. But this is not in the course of events. The experiment has been made, and every time a despot has altered the money . . .

B: Who says anything about altering the money?

F: Why, to force people to take in payment scraps of paper which have been officially baptized *francs,* or to force them to receive, as weighing five grains, a piece of silver which weighs only two and a half, but which has been officially named a *franc,* is the same thing, if not worse; and all the reasoning which can be made in favour of assignats has been made in favour of legal false money. Certainly, looking at it, as you did just now, and as you appear to be doing still, if it is believed that to multiply the instruments of exchange is to multiply the exchanges themselves as well as the things exchanged, it might very reasonably be thought that the most simple means was to double the crowns, and to cause the law to give to the half the name and value of the whole. Well, in both cases, depreciation is inevitable. I think I have told you the cause. I must also inform you, that this depreciation, which, with paper, might go on till it came to nothing, is effected by continually making dupes; and of these, poor people, simple persons, workmen and countrymen are the chief.

B: I see; but stop a little. This dose of Economy is rather too strong for once.

F: Be it so. We are agreed, then, upon this point,—that wealth is the mass of useful things Which we produce by labour; or, still better, the result of all the efforts which we make for the satisfaction of our wants and tastes. These useful things are exchanged for each other, according to the convenience of those to whom they belong. There are two forms in these transactions; one is called barter: in this case, a service is rendered for the sake of receiving an equivalent service immediately. In this form, transactions would be exceedingly limited. In order that they may be multiplied, and accomplished independently of time and space amongst persons unknown to each other, and by infinite fractions, an intermediate agent has been necessary,—this is cash. It gives occasion for exchange, which is nothing else but a complicated bargain. This is what has to be remarked and understood. Exchange decomposes itself into two bargains, into two actors, sale and purchase,—the reunion of which is needed to complete it. You *sell* a service, and receive a crown—then, with this crown, you *buy* a service. Then only is the bargain complete; it is not till then that your effort has been followed by a real satisfaction. Evidently you only work to satisfy the wants of others, that others may work to satisfy yours. So long as you have only the crown which has been given you for your work, you are only entitled to claim the work of another person. When you have done so, the economical evolution will be accomplished as far as you are concerned, since you will then only have obtained, by a real satisfaction, the true reward for your trouble. The idea of a bargain implies a service rendered, and a service received. Why should it not be the same with exchange, which is merely a bargain in two parts? And here there are two observations to be made. First,—It is a very unimportant circumstance whether there be much or little cash in the world. If there is much, much is required; if there is little, little is wanted, for each transaction: that is all. The second observation is this:—Because it is seen that cash always reappears in every exchange, it has come to be regarded as the *sign* and the *measure* of the things exchanged.

B: Will you still deny that cash is the *sign* of the useful things of which you speak?

F: A louis[1] is no more the sign of a sack of corn, than a sack of corn is the sign of a louis.

B: What harm is there in looking at cash as the sign of wealth?

F: The inconvenience is this,—it leads to the idea that we have only to increase the sign, in order to increase the things signified; and we are in danger of adopting all the false measures which you took when I made you an absolute king. We should go still further. Just as in money we see the sign of wealth, we see also in paper money the sign of money; and thence conclude that there is a very easy and simple method of procuring for everybody the pleasures of fortune.

B: But you will not go so far as to dispute that cash is the *measure* of values?

F: Yes, certainly, I do go as far as that, for that is precisely where the illusion lies. It has become customary to refer the value of everything to that of cash. It is said, this is *worth* five, ten, or twenty francs, as we say this *weighs* five, ten, or twenty grains; this *measures* five, ten, or twenty yards; this ground *contains* five, ten, or twenty acres; and hence it has been concluded, that cash is the *measure* of *values.*

B: Well, it appears as if it was so.

F: Yes, it appears so, and it is this I complain of, and not of the reality. A measure of length, size, surface, is a quantity agreed upon, and unchangeable. It is not so with the value of gold and silver. This varies as much as that of corn, wine, cloth, or labour, and from the same causes, for it has the same source and obeys the same laws. Gold is brought within our reach, just like iron, by the labour of miners, the advances of capitalists, and the combination of merchants and seamen. It costs more or less, according to the expense of its production, according to whether there is much or little in the market, and whether it is much or little in request; in a word, it undergoes the fluctuations of all other human productions. But one circumstance is singular, and gives rise to many mistakes.

1. Twenty francs.

When the value of cash varies, the variation is attributed by language to the other productions for which it is exchanged. Thus, let us suppose that all the circumstances relative to gold remain the same, and that the corn harvest has failed. The price of corn will rise. It will be said, "The quarter of corn, which was worth twenty francs, is now worth thirty"; and this will be correct, for it is the value of the corn which has varied, and language agrees with the fact. But let us reverse the supposition: let us suppose that all the circumstances relative to corn remain the same, and that half of all the gold in existence is swallowed up; this time it is the price of gold which will rise. It would seem that we ought to say,—"This Napoleon, which *was worth* twenty francs, *is now worth* forty." Now, do you know how this is expressed? Just as if it was the other objects of comparison which had fallen in price, it is said,—"Corn, which *was worth* twenty francs, *is now only worth* ten."

B: It all comes to the same thing in the end.

F: No doubt; but only think what disturbances, what cheatings are produced in exchanges, when the value of the medium varies, without our becoming aware of it by a change in the name. Old pieces are issued, or notes bearing the name of twenty *francs,* and which will bear that name through every subsequent depreciation. The value will be reduced a quarter, a half, but they will still be called *pieces* or *notes of twenty francs.* Clever persons will take care not to part with their goods unless for a larger number of notes—in other words, they will ask forty francs for what they would formerly have sold for twenty; but simple persons will be taken in. Many years must pass before all the values will find their proper level. Under the influence of ignorance and *custom,* the day's pay of a country labourer will remain for a long time at a franc, while the saleable price of all the articles of consumption around him will be rising. He will sink into destitution without being able to discover the cause. In short, since you wish me to finish, I must beg you, before we separate, to fix your whole attention upon this essential point:—When once false money (under whatever form it may take) is put into circulation, depreciation will ensue, and manifest itself by the universal rise of every thing which is capable of being sold. But this rise in prices is not instantaneous and equal for all things. Sharp men, brokers, and men of business, will not suffer by it; for it is their trade to watch the fluctuations of prices, to observe the cause, and even to speculate upon it. But little tradesmen, countrymen, and workmen, will bear the whole weight of it. The rich man is not any the richer for it, but the poor man becomes poorer by it. Therefore, expedients of this kind have the effect of increasing the distance which separates wealth from poverty, of paralysing the social tendencies which are incessantly bringing men to the same level, and it will require centuries for the suffering classes to regain the ground which they have lost in their advance towards *equality of condition.*

B: Good morning; I shall go and meditate upon the lecture you have been giving me.

F: Have you finished your own dissertation? As for me, I have scarcely begun mine. I have not yet spoken of the *hatred* of capital, of gratuitous credit—a fatal notion, a deplorable mistake, which takes its rise from the same source.

B: What! does this frightful commotion of the populace against capitalists arise from money being confounded with wealth?

F: It is the result of different causes. Unfortunately, certain capitalists have arrogated to themselves monopolies and privileges which are quite sufficient to account for this feeling. But when the theorists of democracy have wished to justify it, to systematize it, to give it the appearance of a reasonable opinion, and to turn it against the very nature of capital, they have had recourse to that false political economy at whose root the same confusion is always to be found. They have said to the people:—"Take a crown, put it under a glass; forget it for a year; then go and look at it, and you will be convinced that it has not produced ten sous, nor five sous, nor any fraction of a sou. Therefore, money produces no interest." Then, substituting for the word money its pretended sign, *capital,* they have made it by their logic undergo this modification—"Then capital produces no interest." Then follow this series of consequences—"Therefore he who lends a capital ought to obtain nothing from it; therefore he who lends you a capital, if he gains something by it, is robbing you; therefore all capitalists are robbers; therefore wealth, which ought to serve gratuitously those who borrow it, belongs in reality to those to whom it does not belong; therefore there is no such thing as property; therefore everything belongs to everybody; therefore . . ."

B: This is very serious; the more so, from the syllogism being so admirably formed. I should very much like to be enlightened on the subject. But, alas! I can no longer command my attention. There is such a confusion in my head of the words *cash, money, services, capital, interest,* that, really, I hardly know where I am. We will, if you please, resume the conversation another day.

F: In the meantime, here is a little work entitled *Capital and Rent.* It may perhaps remove some of your doubts. Just look at it, when you are in want of a little amusement.

B: To amuse me?

F: Who knows? One nail drives in another; one wearisome thing drives away another.

B: I have not yet made up my mind that your views upon cash and political economy in general are correct. But, from your conversation, this is what I have gathered:—That these questions are of the highest importance; for peace or war, order or anarchy, the union or the antagonism of citizens, are at the root of the answer to them. How is it that, in France, a science which concerns us all so nearly, and the diffusion of which would have so decisive an influence upon the fate of mankind, is so little known? Is it that the State does not teach it sufficiently?

F: Not exactly. For, without knowing it, it applies itself to loading everybody's brain with prejudices, and everybody's heart with sentiments favourable to the spirit of anarchy, war, and hatred; so that, when a doctrine of order, peace, and union presents itself, it is in vain that it has clearness and truth on its side,—it cannot gain admittance.

B: Decidedly, you are a frightful grumbler. What interest can the State have in mystifying people's intellects in favour of revolutions, and civil and foreign wars? There must certainly be a great deal of exaggeration in what you say.

F: Consider. At the period when our intellectual faculties begin to develop themselves, at the age when impressions are liveliest, when habits of mind are formed with the greatest ease—when we might look at society and understand it—in a word, as soon as we are seven or eight years old, what does the State do? It puts a bandage over our eyes, takes us gently from the midst of the social circle which surrounds us, to plunge us, with our susceptible faculties, our impressible hearts, into the midst of Roman society. It keeps us there for ten years at least, long enough to make an ineffaceable impression on the brain. Now observe, that Roman society is directly opposed to what our society ought to be. There they lived upon war; here we ought to hate war. There they hated labour; here we ought to live upon labour. There the means of subsistence were founded upon slavery and plunder; here they should be drawn from free industry. Roman society was organised in consequence of its principle. It necessarily admired what made it prosper. There they considered as virtue, what we look upon as vice. Its poets and historians had to exalt what we ought to despise. The very words, *liberty, order, justice, people, honour, influence, &c.,* could not have the same signification at Rome, as they have, or ought to have, at Paris. How can you expect that all these youths who have been at university or conventual schools, with Livy and Quintus Curtius for their catechism, will not understand liberty like the Gracchi, virtue like Cato, patriotism like Caesar? How can you expect them not to be factious and warlike? How can you expect them to take the slightest interest in the mechanism of our social order? Do you think that their minds have been prepared to understand it? Do you not see that, in order to do so, they must get rid of their present impressions, and receive others entirely opposed to them?

F: I will tell you. The most urgent necessity is, not that the State should teach, but that it should *allow* education. All monopolies are detestable, but the worst of all is the monopoly of education.**B:** What do you conclude from that?

www.ingramcontent.com/pod-product-compliance
Lightning Source LLC
LaVergne TN
LVHW100201061126
851857LV00010B/347